How To Integrate BCS with Search in SharePoint 2013

STEVEN MANN

How To Integrate BCS with Search in SharePoint 2013

Copyright © 2013 by Steven Mann

Trademarks

Screenshots of Microsoft Products and Services

Warning and Disclaimer

Introduction

This guide steps you through the process of incorporating external data into SharePoint 2013 Search by leveraging Business Data Connectivity Services (BCS). It provides an end-to-end solution that integrates product data from a SQL Server database into SharePoint by using external content types. Creating a new search vertical as well as customizing the display and hover panels of the business data search results is also covered.

Reference links and source code are available on www.stevethemanmann.com:

Step 1: Prepare the Data Source

The scenario and sample data for this guide uses Product information from the

AdventureWorks2012 sample database in SQL Server.

The first step is to create your read list and read item procedures.

Create a stored procedure that returns all of the information you
want to search and make sure all rows are returned:

```sql
-- CREATE PROCEDURE GetAllProductsforBC
   AS
-- BEGIN
      -- SET NOCOUNT ON added to prevent extra result sets from
      -- interfering with SELECT statements.
      SET NOCOUNT ON;

      -- Insert statements for procedure here
      SELECT
         p.ProductID,
         p.ProductNumber,
         p.Name AS ProductName,
         p.Class AS ProductClass,
         p.Color AS ProductColor,
         p.ProductLine,
         p.ListPrice AS ProductListPrice,
         pc.Name AS ProductCategory,
         psc.Name AS ProductSubCategory,
         pm.Name AS ProductModel,
         pd.Description as ProductDescription
      FROM Production.Product p
```

	ProductID	ProductNumber	ProductName	ProductClass	ProductColor	ProductLine	ProductListPrice	ProductCategory	ProductSubCategory	ProductModel	ProductDescription
1	994	BB-7421	LL Bottom Bracket	L	NULL	NULL	53.99	Components	Bottom Brackets	LL Bottom Bracket	Chromoly steel.
2	995	BB-8107	ML Bottom Bracket	M	NULL	NULL	101.24	Components	Bottom Brackets	ML Bottom Bracket	Aluminum alloy cups; large d
3	996	BB-9108	HL Bottom Bracket	H	NULL	NULL	121.49	Components	Bottom Brackets	HL Bottom Bracket	Aluminum alloy cups; and a H
4	984	BK-M18S-40	Mountain-500 Silver, 40	L	Silver	M	564.99	Bikes	Mountain Bikes	Mountain-500	Suitable for any type of riding
5	985	BK-M18S-42	Mountain-500 Silver, 42	L	Silver	M	564.99	Bikes	Mountain Bikes	Mountain-500	Suitable for any type of riding
6	986	BK-M18S-44	Mountain-500 Silver, 44	L	Silver	M	564.99	Bikes	Mountain Bikes	Mountain-500	Suitable for any type of riding
7	987	BK-M18S-48	Mountain-500 Silver, 48	L	Silver	M	564.99	Bikes	Mountain Bikes	Mountain-500	Suitable for any type of riding
8	988	BK-M18S-52	Mountain-500 Silver, 52	L	Silver	M	564.99	Bikes	Mountain Bikes	Mountain-500	Suitable for any type of riding
9	989	BK-M18B-40	Mountain-500 Black, 40	L	Black	M	539.99	Bikes	Mountain Bikes	Mountain-500	Suitable for any type of riding
10	990	BK-M18B-42	Mountain-500 Black, 42	L	Black	M	539.99	Bikes	Mountain Bikes	Mountain-500	Suitable for any type of riding
11	991	BK-M18B-44	Mountain-500 Black, 44	L	Black	M	539.99	Bikes	Mountain Bikes	Mountain-500	Suitable for any type of riding
12	992	BK-M18B-48	Mountain-500 Black, 48	L	Black	M	539.99	Bikes	Mountain Bikes	Mountain-500	Suitable for any type of riding
13	993	BK-M18B-52	Mountain-500 Black, 52	L	Black	M	539.99	Bikes	Mountain Bikes	Mountain-500	Suitable for any type of riding
14	980	BK-M38S-38	Mountain-400-W Silver, 38	M	Silver	M	769.49	Bikes	Mountain Bikes	Mountain-400-W	This bike delivers a high-leve

I created a GetAllProductsForBCS stored procedure which returns the product information I need using several joins:

```sql
CREATE PROCEDURE GetAllProductsForBCS
AS
BEGIN
        -- SET NOCOUNT ON added to prevent extra result sets
from
        -- interfering with SELECT statements.
        SET NOCOUNT ON;

    -- Insert statements for procedure here
        SELECT
                p.ProductID,
                p.ProductNumber,
                p.Name AS ProductName,
                p.Class AS ProductClass,
                p.Color AS ProductColor,
                p.ProductLine,
                p.ListPrice AS ProductListPrice,
                pc.Name AS ProductCategory,
                psc.Name AS ProductSubCategory,
                pm.Name AS ProductModel,
                pd.Description as ProductDescription
        FROM Production.Product p
                INNER JOIN Production.ProductSubcategory psc
                        ON psc.ProductSubcategoryID =
p.ProductSubcategoryID
                INNER JOIN Production.ProductCategory pc
                        ON pc.ProductCategoryID =
psc.ProductCategoryID
                INNER JOIN Production.ProductModel pm
                        on pm.ProductModelID = p.ProductModelID
                INNER JOIN Produc-
tion.ProductModelProductDescriptionCulture pmx
                        ON pm.ProductModelID = pmx.ProductModelID
                INNER JOIN Production.ProductDescription pd
                        ON pmx.ProductDescriptionID =
pd.ProductDescriptionID
        WHERE pmx.CultureID='en'
```

This procedure is used to create a ReadList method in the External Content Type.

Create a stored procedure that returns the same information but only for a particular entity by using the ID as a parameter:

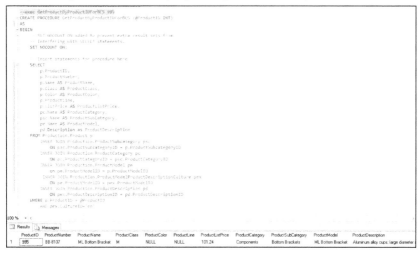

Make sure only 1 row is returned for a given identity.

I created a GetAllProductsForBCS stored procedure which returns the product information I need based on the passed in ProductID parameter:

```
CREATE PROCEDURE GetProductByProductIDForBCS (@ProductID INT)
AS
BEGIN
        -- SET NOCOUNT ON added to prevent extra result sets
from
        -- interfering with SELECT statements.
        SET NOCOUNT ON;

    -- Insert statements for procedure here
        SELECT
                p.ProductID,
                p.ProductNumber,
                p.Name AS ProductName,
                p.Class AS ProductClass,
                p.Color AS ProductColor,
                p.ProductLine,
                p.ListPrice AS ProductListPrice,
                pc.Name AS ProductCategory,
                psc.Name AS ProductSubCategory,
                pm.Name AS ProductModel,
                pd.Description as ProductDescription
        FROM Production.Product p
```

```sql
                INNER JOIN Production.ProductSubcategory psc
                    ON psc.ProductSubcategoryID =
p.ProductSubcategoryID
                INNER JOIN Production.ProductCategory pc
                    ON pc.ProductCategoryID =
psc.ProductCategoryID
                INNER JOIN Production.ProductModel pm
                    on pm.ProductModelID = p.ProductModelID
                INNER JOIN Produc-
tion.ProductModelProductDescriptionCulture pmx
                    ON pm.ProductModelID = pmx.ProductModelID
                INNER JOIN Production.ProductDescription pd
                    ON pmx.ProductDescriptionID =
pd.ProductDescriptionID
        WHERE p.ProductID = @ProductID
                AND pmx.CultureID='en'
```

This procedure is used to create a ReadItem method in the External Content Type. The SELECT statement here should be exactly the same as the SELECT in the ReadList. The only difference here is that additional WHERE condition for the passed in @ProductID.

Step 2: Add Credentials to the Secure Store Service

In order for the External Content Type to be created and BCS to access your external data source, the data source credentials need to be stored. The Secure Store Service in SharePoint allows you to store credentials. For this scenario, a SQL database account was created named "AWDBAccount". Therefore an entry in the Secure Store Service needs to be added for SQL Authentication.

Navigate to Central Administration and click on Manage Service Applications under the Application Management section:

Click on the Secure Store Service application link:

Search Administration Web Service for Search Service Application

Search Service Application

    Search Service Application Proxy

Secure Store Service

    Secure Store Service

Security Token Service Application

User Profile App

    User Profile App

WSS_UsageApplication

    WSS_UsageApplication

If you do not have a Secure Store Service listed, you'll need to create one.

If you see a message at the top of the screen regarding a key, click the Generate New Key button from the top ribbon:

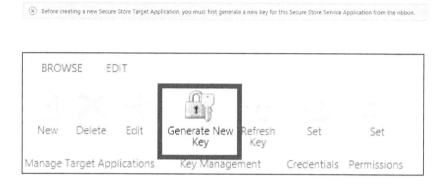

Enter a pass phrase and click OK:

Click New from the top ribbon:

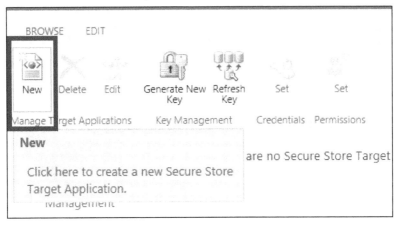

Enter a Target Application ID, Display Name, and Contact E-mail:

You will need the Target Application ID to create the External Content Type. Click Next.

Change the Windows User Name field name to User ID the Windows Password field name to Password.

Change the associated Field Types from to User Name and Password. Click Next.

Enter Target Application Administrators and click OK:

The Target Application entry is created:

Select the Target Application checkbox and click the Set Credentials button:

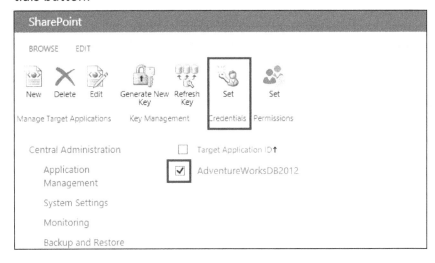

Enter the Credential Owner (this should be the service account that runs BCS), enter the SQL database User ID and Password. Click OK:

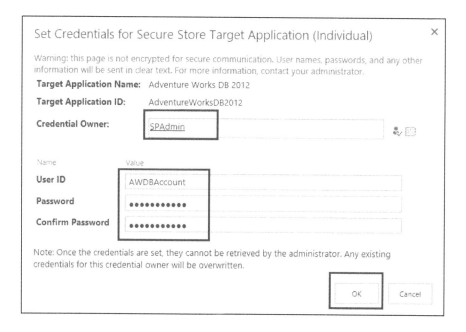

Step 3: Create an External Content Type

The methods here describe the steps for a no-code solution in creating an External Content Type that uses your data source as the provider of information via SharePoint Designer 2013.

Launch SharePoint Designer 2013 and open your Search Center site:

Click the External Content Types from the Site Objects and then click the External Content Type button from the top-ribbon:

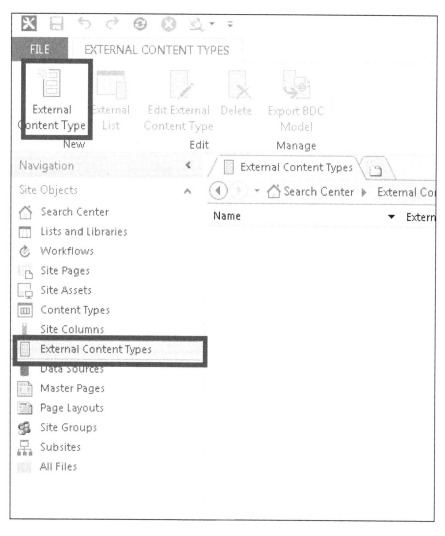

Enter a Name and Display Name and then click on the External System link:

Click on the Add Connection button:

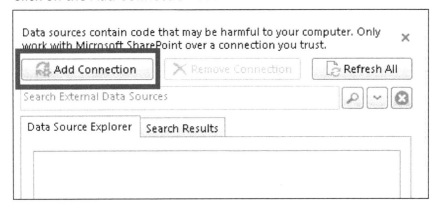

Select the type of connection. For this example, SQL Server is being used:

Click OK.

Enter the Database Server, the Database Name, and select Connect with Impersonated Custom Identity. Enter the Secure Store Application ID that was created in the previous section:

Click OK. If prompted, enter the **SQL Server credentials** to access the database.

Expand the database in the Data Source Explorer tab and then expand the Routines folder. Locate the Read List procedure, right click and select New Read List Operation:

Enter an Operation Name and Display Name.

The Operation Name becomes a prefix (ReadList.propertyname) in the crawled properties so it is a good idea to include an entity description in the name, otherwise it would be hard to distinguish crawled properties from their external content types.

Click Next. The example does not limit the Read List items and thus there are no Input Parameters. Click Next:

On the Return Parameter Configuration screen, make sure the row identifier (primary key) is selected and check the Map to

Identifier checkbox. The Identifier, Field, and DisplayName become populated with the row identifier. Click Finish.

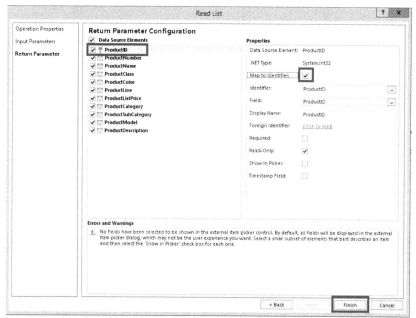

Next, locate the Read Item procedure, right click and select New
Read Item Operation:

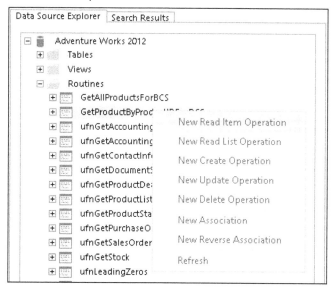

Enter appropriate operation names. Click Next:

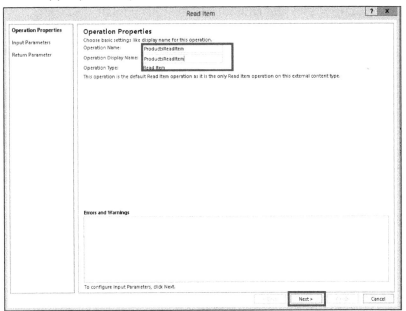

On the Input Parameters Configuration screen, make sure the input parameter is selected and the Map to Identifier is checked. Click Next:

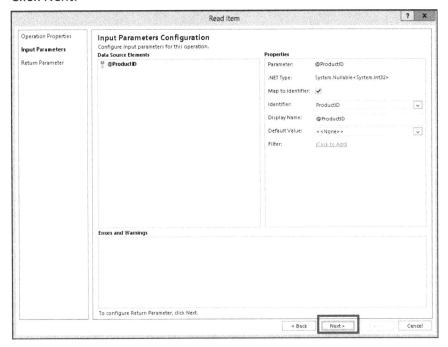

On the Return Parameter Configuration screen, make sure the row identifier (primary key) is selected and check the Map to Identifier checkbox. The Identifier, Field, and DisplayName become populated with the row identifier. Click Finish.

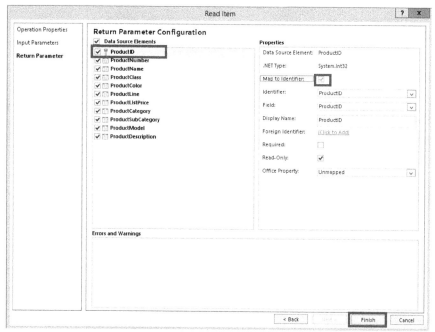

The new operations appear in the External Content Type Operations section:

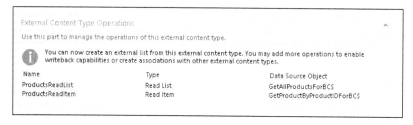

Save the External Content Type:

Keep SharePoint Designer 2013 open to the External Content Type. Navigate to your Business Data Connectivity Service Application and verify the new external content type exists:

In your Business Data Connectivity Service Application, click the Configure button.

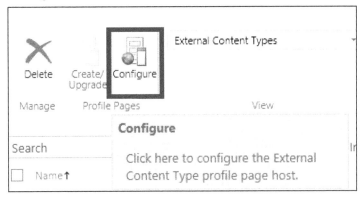

Enter a location to host the External Content Type profile pages:

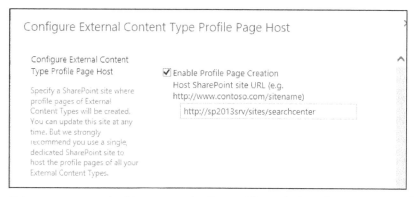

It is recommended to use a dedicate SharePoint site. I personally like things being all together in my Search Center Site Collection so I use that.

Scroll down and click OK.

While you are here you could set the permissions in the BCS for the External Content type as explained in the next section (or just come back to it).

Navigate back to SharePoint Designer 2013 and with the External Content Type opened, click on the Create Profile Page button from the top-ribbon:

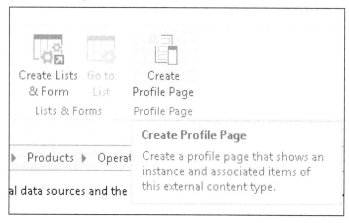

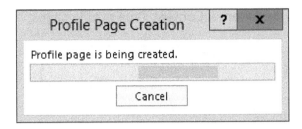

The Profile Page is created. This page becomes used for the search results URL if a custom URL (page) is not used as part of the data source.

Step 4: Set Permissions on the BCS Entity

Navigate to your Business Data Connectivity Service Application and select the External Content Type by checking the checkbox:

Click on the Set Object Permissions button from the top-ribbon.

Enter accounts into the account box (if your external content type is for general use include Everyone):

Click Add. Select each added account and check off the appropriate permissions. For Everyone, only check off Execute and Selectable In Clients.

Set Object Permissions

To add an account, or group, type or select it below and click 'Add'.

	Add

SPSearch
AD2012\administrator

To remove an account, or group, select it above and click 'Remove'. — [Remove]

Permissions for SPSearch:

- Edit ☑
- Execute ☑
- Selectable In Clients ☑
- Set Permissions ☐

☑ Propagate permissions to all methods of this external content type. Doing so will overwrite existing permissions.

[OK] [Cancel]

Click OK.

Step 5: Create a Content Source for the External Content Type

Navigate to Central Administration and click on Manage service applications:

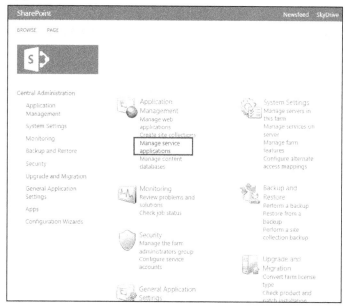

Click on the Search Service Application:

Click on Content Sources under Crawling (in the left hand column):

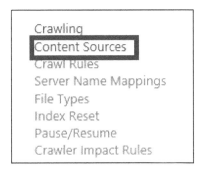

On the Manage Content Source page click the New Content Source link:

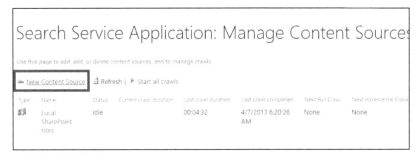

Enter a name for the Content Source and select Line of Business Data. Select the Crawl selected external data source and check off the data source:

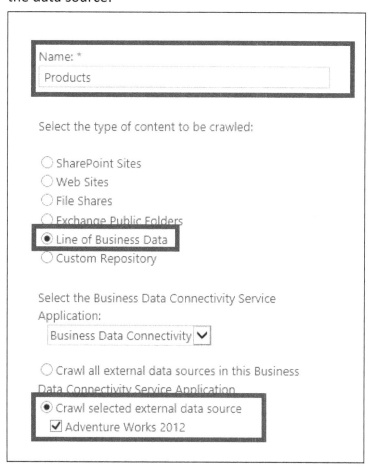

Scroll down and click OK.

The content source is created and listed on the Manage Content Sources page:

Hover over the new content source and click the drop-down menu. Select Start Full Crawl:

Step 6: Create Managed Properties Based on Crawled Properties

After the crawl has completed, you now need to create managed properties and map them to the crawled properties from the new content source. This may be accomplished from the Search Service Application UI or from PowerShell. Either way, you need to know what crawled properties have been created.

From the Search Service Application, click on Search Schema on the left hand side of the screen under Queries and Results:

On the Managed Properties page, click on Crawled Properties at the top:

Select Business Data from the Category drop-down and click the filter button:

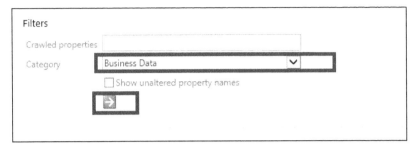

The crawled properties from the external data source are displayed:

You may also use PowerShell to list out the crawled properties. I use the following commands:

Add-PSSnapin Microsoft.SharePoint.PowerShell -ErrorAction SilentlyContinue

$ssa = Get-SPEnterpriseSearchServiceApplication

Get-SPEnterpriseSearchMetadataCrawledProperty -SearchApplication $ssa -Category 'Business Data' | ft Name

```
Administrator: Windows PowerShell                                    _ □ x
PS C:\> Add-PSSnapin Microsoft.SharePoint.PowerShell -ErrorAction SilentlyContinue
PS C:\>
PS C:\> $ssa = Get-SPEnterpriseSearchServiceApplication
PS C:\>
PS C:\>
PS C:\> Get-SPEnterpriseSearchMetadataCrawledProperty -SearchApplication $ssa -Category 'Business Data' | ft Name

Name
----
docaclmeta
EntityName
EntityNamespace
ProductsReadListElement.ProductCategory
ProductsReadListElement.ProductClass
ProductsReadListElement.ProductColor
ProductsReadListElement.ProductDescription
ProductsReadListElement.ProductID
ProductsReadListElement.ProductLine
ProductsReadListElement.ProductListPrice
ProductsReadListElement.ProductModel
ProductsReadListElement.ProductName
ProductsReadListElement.ProductNumber
ProductsReadListElement.ProductSubCategory


PS C:\> _
```

Now that you know what the crawled properties are, you can map them to managed properties. If the managed properties were already created, you could simply click on each crawled property on the Crawled Property page and map them. In this case, there are no managed properties yet.

Therefore click on the Managed Properties link at the top of the Crawled Properties page:

Search Service Application: Crawled Properties

Managed Properties | Crawled Properties | Categories

On the Managed Properties page, click on New Managed Property:

Enter a name for the property. I usually prefix them with the entity type so they are all displayed together and I know which content source they are from. Select the Type and check the Searchable checkbox:

Scroll down and check Queryable and Retrievable. For this example, the Product Category will be refinable and sortable so I selected "Yes -active" for both of those entries:

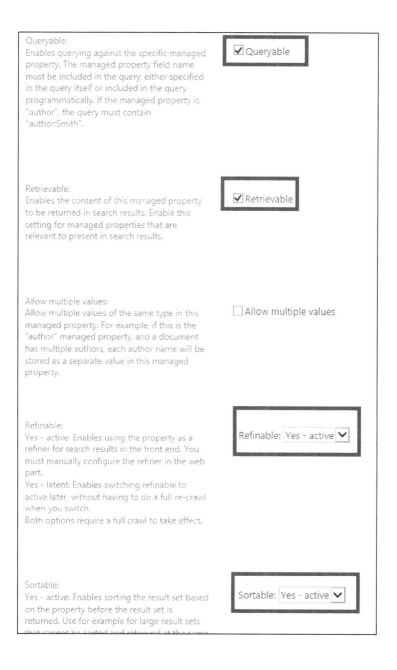

Queryable:
Enables querying against the specific managed property. The managed property field name must be included in the query, either specified in the query itself or included in the query programmatically. If the managed property is "author", the query must contain "author:Smith".

☑ Queryable

Retrievable:
Enables the content of this managed property to be returned in search results. Enable this setting for managed properties that are relevant to present in search results.

☑ Retrievable

Allow multiple values:
Allow multiple values of the same type in this managed property. For example, if this is the "author" managed property, and a document has multiple authors, each author name will be stored as a separate value in this managed property.

☐ Allow multiple values

Refinable:
Yes - active: Enables using the property as a refiner for search results in the front end. You must manually configure the refiner in the web part.
Yes - latent: Enables switching refinable to active later, without having to do a full re-crawl when you switch.
Both options require a full crawl to take effect.

Refinable: Yes - active ▾

Sortable:
Yes - active: Enables sorting the result set based on the property before the result set is returned. Use for example for large result sets

Sortable: Yes - active ▾

For external content I usually select Include content from the first crawled property setting. These should be one-to-one mappings so it really doesn't make a difference. Click on the Add Mapping button:

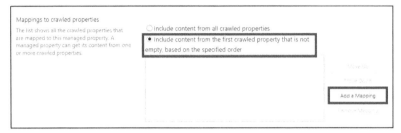

In the Crawled property dialog, select Business Data from the filter drop-down. Select the appropriate crawled property and click OK.

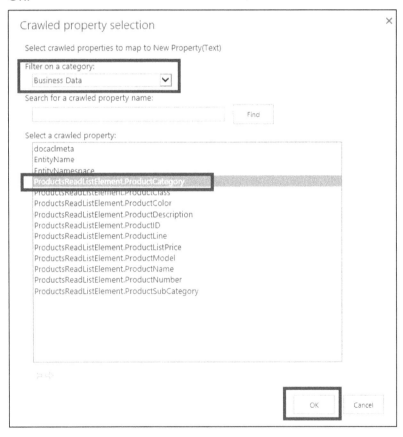

Back on the Add Managed Property page, click OK:

These managed properties are configured to be searchable, queryable, retrievable, sortable and refinable.	☐ Word Part Extraction - Custom5
	☐ Word Exact Extraction - Custom
	☐ Word Part Exact Extraction - Custom
	OK Cancel

You'll need to repeat this process for each crawled property.

Performing the mapping through the UI can become tedious. That's why I create a script to map all of my properties:

```
Add-PSSnapin Microsoft.SharePoint.PowerShell -ErrorAction SilentlyContinue
$ssa = Get-SPEnterpriseSearchServiceApplication

$crawledProperty = Get-SPEnterpriseSearchMetadataCrawledProperty -SearchApplication $ssa -Name ProductsReadListElement.ProductCategory
$managedProperty = New-SPEnterpriseSearchMetadataManagedProperty -SearchApplication $ssa -Name ProductCategory -FullTextQueriable:$true -Queryable:$true -Retrievable:$true -Type 1
New-SPEnterpriseSearchMetadataMapping -SearchApplication $ssa -ManagedProperty $managedProperty -CrawledProperty $crawledProperty
```

Just repeat the last three lines for each property mapping.

There are no parameters for sortable or refinable so I just go into the UI and change those settings manually for the properties I want to sort on or refine. You could create the crawled property if you knew what it was going to be named but in my script I get the crawled property since it was already created.

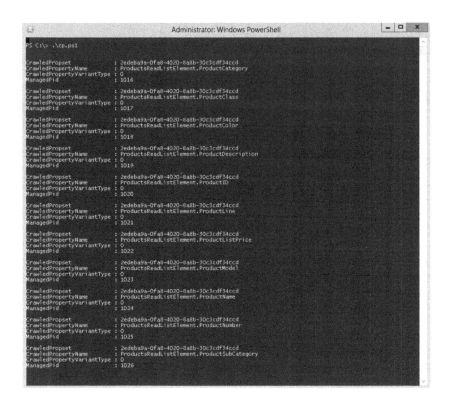

In order for the Managed Properties to take effect, you now need to run a full crawl on the content source again.

Step 7: Create a Result Source for the New Content Source

Navigate to your Search Center and select Site Settings from the Settings menu:

Under the Site Collection Administration section, click on Search Result Sources:

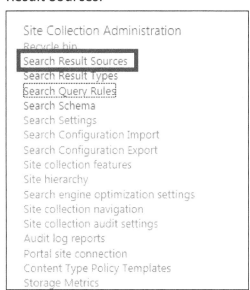

On the Manage Result Sources page, click on the New Result Source link:

On the Add Result Source page, enter a name for the Result Source. For this example, I am using Products:

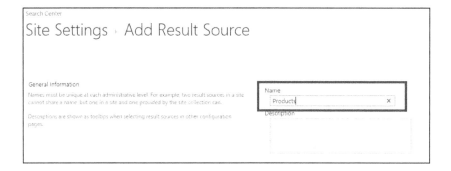

Scroll down and click on the Launch Query Builder button:

In the Property Filter section, first select "--Show all managed properties--":

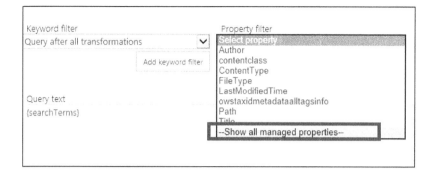

Next select ContentSource from the drop-down. Select Equals and Manual value:

Enter the name of the content source (e.g. Products) in the text box and click Add property filter:

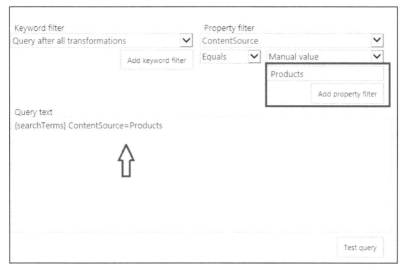

The property filter is added to the Query text. Click OK on the Build Your Query dialog.

The property filter is added to the Query Transform text box.

Click Save:

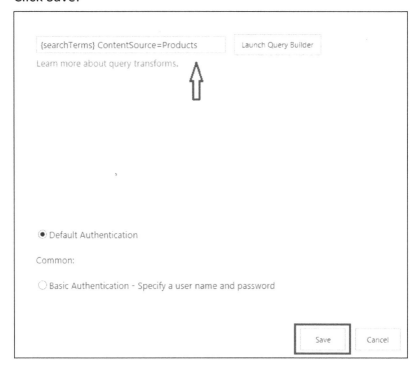

The new result source is created and appears under the Defined for this site section:

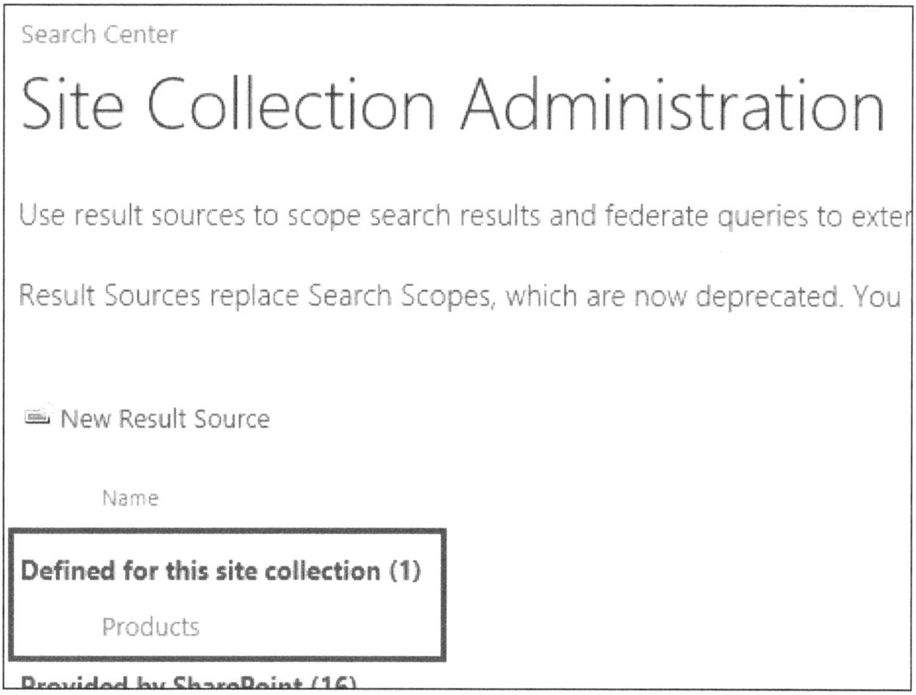

Search Center

Site Collection Administration

Use result sources to scope search results and federate queries to exter

Result Sources replace Search Scopes, which are now deprecated. You

New Result Source

Name

Defined for this site collection (1)

Products

Provided by SharePoint (16)

Step 8: Create a Result Type for the Result Source

Navigate to your Search Center and select Site Settings from the Settings menu.

Under the Site Collection Administration section, click on the Search Result Types link:

Site Collection Administration
Recycle bin
Search Result Sources
Search Result Types
Search Query Rules
Search Schema
Search Settings
Search Configuration Import
Search Configuration Export
Site collection features
Site hierarchy
Search engine optimization settings
Site collection navigation

On the Result Types page click on the New Result Type link:

Enter a name for the Result Type. Select the Result Source created in the previous section from the source drop-down. Skip the types of content rule. Select Default Item for now under "What should these results look like?". You will create a custom item template in later sections.

Site Collection Administration › Add Result Type

apply to all sites in the site collection. To make one for just this site, use site result types.

Give it a name

| Products |

Which source should results match?

| Products ▾ |

What types of content should match? You can skip this rule to match all content

| Select a value ▾ |

Add value

What should these results look like?

| Default Item ▾ |

Note: This result type will automatically update with the latest properties in your display template each time you visit the Manage Result Types Page.

Display template URL

~~/sitecollection_catalogs/masterpage/display Templates/Search/Item_Default~~

☐ Optimize for frequent use

| Save | | Cancel |

Click Save.

Step 9: Create a Search Results Page for the New Content Source

Navigate to your Search Center and select Site Contents from the Settings menu:

Locate and double-click the Pages library:

From the Files tab in the top ribbon, select Page from the New Document drop-down menu:

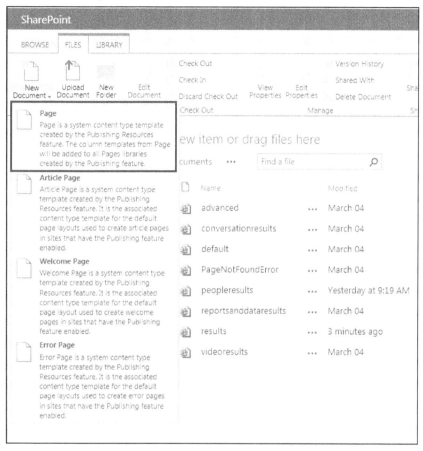

On the Create Page page, enter a title and URL Name. Click Create.

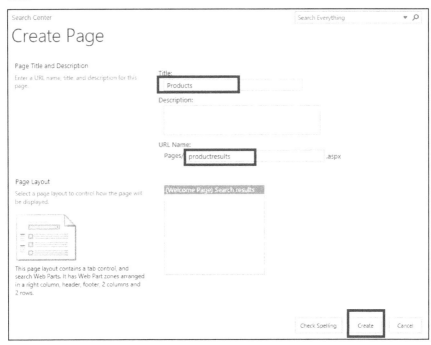

Select the ellipsis menu on the new page and click on OPEN:

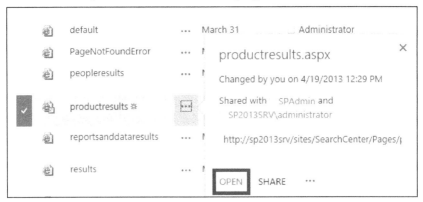

From the Settings menu select Edit page:

Locate the Search Results web part and select Edit Web Part from the drop-down menu:

In the Properties tool pane that appeared on the right, click the Change query button:

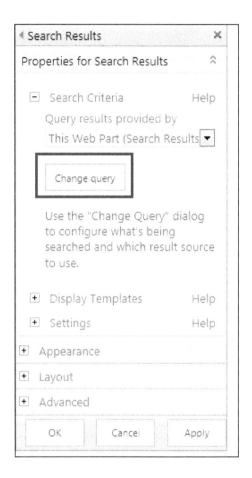

The Build Your Query dialog appears.

In the Select a query section, select the custom Result Source created in the previous section of this chapter:

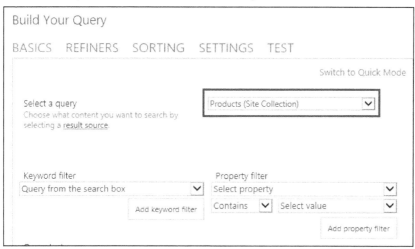

Click OK on the Build Your Query dialog.

Click OK in the web part properties tool pane:

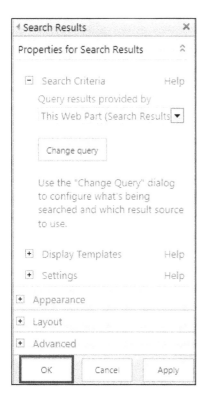

Check in the page:

Checked out to you Only you can see your recent changes. Check it in.

Publish the page:

Recent draft not published Visitors can't see recent changes. Publish this draft.

Step 10: Add a Custom Results Page to the Search Center Navigation

Navigate to your Search Center and select Site Settings from the Settings menu:

Under the Search section click the Search Settings link:

At the bottom the Search Settings page, click on Add Link...:

Enter a title and the URL to the custom page that was created in the previous section. Click OK.

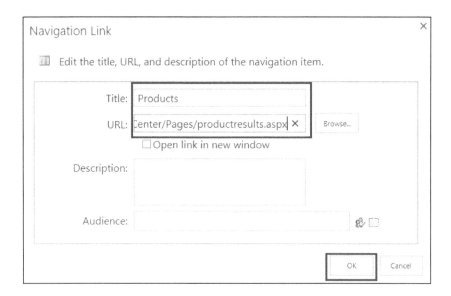

Back on the Search Settings page click OK:

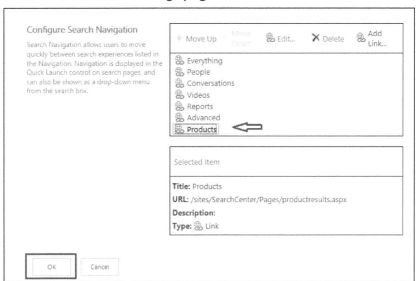

Configure Search Navigation

Search Navigation allows users to move quickly between search experiences listed in the Navigation. Navigation is displayed in the Quick Launch control on search pages, and can also be shown as a drop-down menu from the search box.

Move Up   Move Down   Edit...   ✕ Delete   Add Link...

- Everything
- People
- Conversations
- Videos
- Reports
- Advanced
- Products

Selected Item

Title: Products
URL: /sites/SearchCenter/Pages/productresults.aspx
Description:
Type: Link

OK   Cancel

Step 11: Test the Results

Navigate to your Search Center. The new navigation item appears at the top. Click on the new link and perform a search:

The results aren't too pretty. The next section explains how to create custom item templates and hover panels for the external content source.

Step 12: Create an Item Display Template

Fire up SharePoint Designer 2013 and Open the Search Center Site:

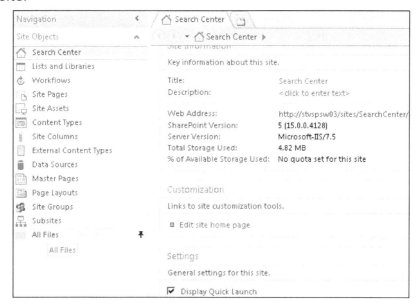

Click on All Files from the left-hand navigation:

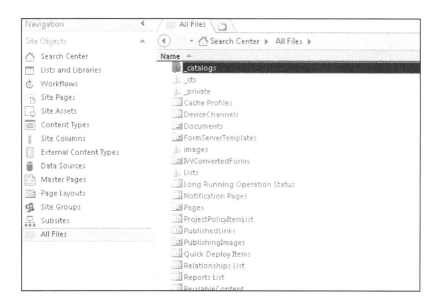

A list of all files is displayed in the main window.

If you attempt to get the files from the Master Pages object, you will not see any items once you get to the Display Templates folders.

Double-click on the _catalogs folder in the main window
This action displays the _catalogs structure under the left-hand navigation.

Expand the _catalogs folder, then the masterpage folder, and then the Display Templates folder.

Click on the Search folder under Display Templates:

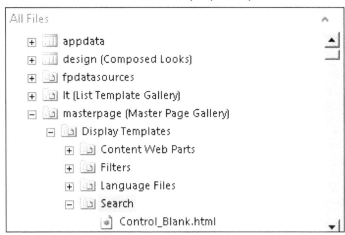

The list of Search display templates is shown in the main window area.

Locate Item_Default.html and Item_Default.js. Select both files, right-click, and select copy:

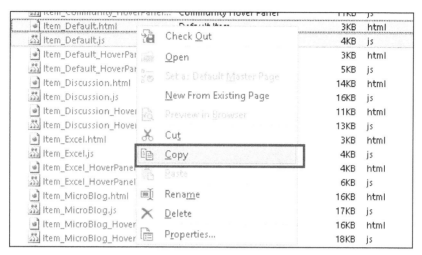

Right click again and select Paste:

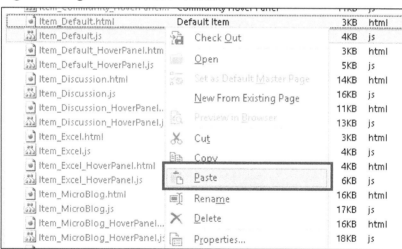

The files are copied in place.

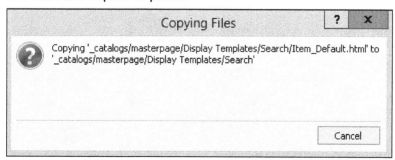

Rename the html copy:

Item_Default.html	Default Item	
Item_Default.js	Default Item	
Item_Product.html	Default Item	
Item_Default_copy(1).js	Default Item	
Item_Default_HoverPanel.html	Default Hover Panel	
Item_Default_HoverPanel.js	Default Hover Panel	

SharePoint automatically renames the .js file:

Item_PowerPoint_HoverPane...	PowerPoint Hover Panel	10KB	js
Item_Product.html	Default Item	3KB	html
Item_Product.js	Default Item	4KB	js
Item_Reply.html	Reply Item	14KB	html
Item_Reply.js	Reply Item	15KB	js

Right-click the html file and select Edit File in Advanced Mode:

Rename the title:

```
1  <html xmlns:mso="urn:schemas-microsoft-com:office:office" xmlns:
2  <head>
3  <title>Product Item</title>          <===
4
5  <!--[if gte mso 9]><xml>
6  <mso:CustomDocumentProperties>
7  <mso:TemplateHidden msdt:dt="string">0</mso:TemplateHidden>
```

Add the external content type managed properties to the Man-agedProperties tag:

'ProductSubCategory':'ProductSubCategory','ProductN
umber':'ProductNumber',

(see code examples on www.SteveTheManMann.com)

In the javascript code block, rename the hover panel:

```
if(!$isNull(ctx.CurrentItem) && !$isNull(ctx.ClientControl)){
    var id = ctx.ClientControl.get_nextUniqueId();
    var itemId = id + Srch.U.Ids.item;
    var hoverId = id + Srch.U.Ids.hover;
    var hoverUrl = "~sitecollection/_catalogs/masterpage/Display Templates/Search/Item_Product_HoverPanel.js";
    $setResultItem(itemId, ctx.CurrentItem);
    if(ctx.CurrentItem.IsContainer){
        ctx.CurrentItem.csr_Icon = Srch.U.getFolderIconUrl();
    }
    ctx.currentItem_ShowHoverPanelCallback = Srch.U.getShowHoverPanelCallback(itemId, hoverId, hoverUrl);
    ctx.currentItem_HideHoverPanelCallback = Srch.U.getHideHoverPanelCallback();
```

You will create the hover panel file in the next section.

Rename the data-displaytemplate:

```
<div id="_#= $htmlEncode(itemId) =#_" name="Item" data-displaytemplate="ProductItem" class=
    _#=ctx.RenderBody(ctx)=#_
    <div id="_#= $htmlEncode(hoverId) =#_" class="ms-srch-hover-outerContainer"></div>
</div>
```

In the javascript code block, I create variables that determine if there is data in the managed property fields:

```
;'--#_
    if(!$isNull(ctx.CurrentItem) && !$isNull(ctx.ClientControl)){
        var id = ctx.ClientControl.get_nextUniqueId();
        var itemId = id + Srch.U.Ids.item;
        var hoverId = id + Srch.U.Ids.hover;
        var hoverUrl = "~sitecollection/_catalogs/masterpage/Display Templates/Search/Item_Product_HoverPanel.js";
        $setResultItem(itemId, ctx.CurrentItem);
        if(ctx.CurrentItem.IsContainer){
            ctx.CurrentItem.csr_Icon = Srch.U.getFolderIconUrl();
        }

        var has_name = !$isEmptyString(ctx.CurrentItem.ProductName);
        var has_model = !$isEmptyString(ctx.CurrentItem.ProductModel);
        var has_number = !$isEmptyString(ctx.CurrentItem.ProductNumber);
        var has_category = !$isEmptyString(ctx.CurrentItem.ProductCategory);

        ctx.currentItem_ShowHoverPanelCallback = Srch.U.getShowHoverPanelCallback(itemId, hoverId, hoverUrl);
        ctx.currentItem_HideHoverPanelCallback = Srch.U.getHideHoverPanelCallback();
    }
#-->
```

var has_name = !$isEmptyString(ctx.CurrentItem.ProductName);

var has_model = !$isEmptyString(ctx.CurrentItem.ProductModel);

var has_number = !$isEmptyString(ctx.CurrentItem.ProductNumber);

var has_category = !$isEmptyString(ctx.CurrentItem.ProductCategory);

Remove the ctx.RenderBody line:

```
                <div id="_#= $htmlEncode(itemId) =#_" name="It
                _#=ctx.RenderBody(ctx)=#_
                    <div id="_#= $htmlEncode(hoverId) =#_" cla
            </div>
:!--#_
        }
#-->
```

For each managed property, create a code block similar to the following:

```
<!--#
            if(has_number == true) {
 #-->
                <div id="ProductNumberField">
                    <div id="ProductNumberValue" class="ms-srch-ellipsis" title="_#=
ctx.CurrentItem.ProductNumber =#_">Product Number:_#=
ctx.CurrentItem.ProductNumber =#_ </div>
                </div>
<!--#
            }
 #-->
```

Code examples are available on www.SteveTheManMann.com.

Save the html file.

Step 13: Create an Item Hover Panel

Back in the listing of display templates, locate and select the Item_Default_HoverPanel files. Right-click and select Copy:

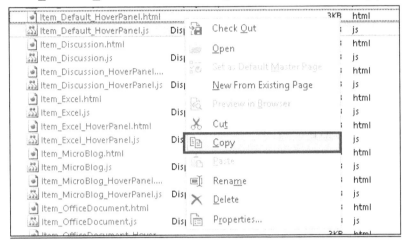

Right-click again and select Paste:

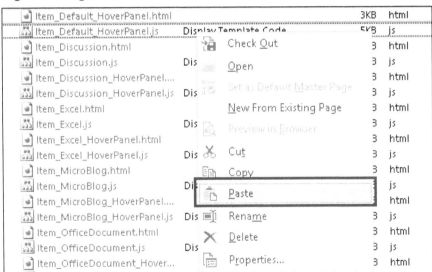

Rename the html file:

SharePoint automatically renames the .js file:

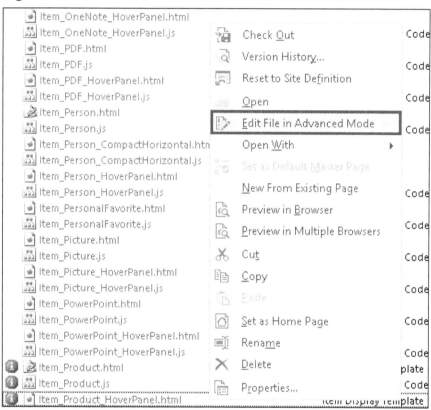

🔵	Item_Product.html	Item Display Template
🔵	Item_Product.js	Display Template Code
🔵	Item_Product_HoverPanel.html	Item Display Template
🔵	Item_Product_HoverPanel.js	Display Template Code

Right click the html file and select Edit File in Advanced Mode:

Files	Menu	
Item_OneNote_HoverPanel.html		
Item_OneNote_HoverPanel.js	Check Out	Code
Item_PDF.html	Version History...	
Item_PDF.js	Reset to Site Definition	Code
Item_PDF_HoverPanel.html	Open	Code
Item_PDF_HoverPanel.js		
Item_Person.html	Edit File in Advanced Mode	Code
Item_Person.js	Open With ▶	
Item_Person_CompactHorizontal.htn	Set as Default Master Page	
Item_Person_CompactHorizontal.js	New From Existing Page	Code
Item_Person_HoverPanel.html		
Item_Person_HoverPanel.js	Preview in Browser	
Item_PersonalFavorite.html	Preview in Multiple Browsers	Code
Item_PersonalFavorite.js		
Item_Picture.html	Cut	Code
Item_Picture.js		
Item_Picture_HoverPanel.html	Copy	Code
Item_Picture_HoverPanel.js	Paste	
Item_PowerPoint.html	Set as Home Page	Code
Item_PowerPoint.js		
Item_PowerPoint_HoverPanel.html	Rename	Code
Item_PowerPoint_HoverPanel.js		
Item_Product.html	Delete	plate
Item_Product.js	Properties...	Code
Item_Product_HoverPanel.html		Item Display Template

Rename the title:

```
1 <html xmlns:mso="urn:schemas-microsoft-com:office:office"
2 <head>
3 <title>Product Hover Panel</title>
4
5 <!--[if gte mso 9]><xml>
6 <mso:CustomDocumentProperties>
```

Copy and paste the ManagedPropertyMapping from the item display template created in the previous section:

```
<!--[if gte mso 9]><xml>
<mso:CustomDocumentProperties>
<mso:TemplateHidden msdt:dt="string">0</mso:TemplateHidden>
<mso:MasterPageDescription msdt:dt="string">Displays the default hover panel template.</mso:MasterPageDescription>
<mso:ContentTypeId msdt:dt="string">0x0101002039C03B61C64EC4A04F5361F385106603</mso:ContentTypeId>
<mso:TargetControlType msdt:dt="string">;#SearchHoverPanel;#</mso:TargetControlType>
<mso:HtmlDesignAssociated msdt:dt="string">1</mso:HtmlDesignAssociated>
<mso:ManagedPropertyMapping msdt:dt="string">'ProductSubCategory':'ProductSubCategory','ProductNumber':
'Title':'Title','Path':'Path','Description':'Description','EditorOWSUSER':
<mso:HtmlDesignConversionSucceeded msdt:dt="string">True</mso:HtmlDesignConversionSucceeded>
<mso:HtmlDesignStatusAndPreview msdt:dt="string">http://sp2013srv/sites/SearchCenter/_catalogs/masterpage/Display%20Templates/Search
</mso:CustomDocumentProperties>
```

Rename the Default entries:

```
<body>
    <div id="Item_Product_HoverPanel">
<!--#
        var i = 0;
        var id = ctx.CurrentItem.csr_id;
        ctx.CurrentItem.csr_ShowViewLibrary = !Srch.U.isWebPage(ctx.CurrentItem.FileExtension);
        if (ctx.CurrentItem.IsContainer)
        {
            ctx.CurrentItem.csr_FileType = Srch.Res.ct_Folder
        }
        ctx.CurrentItem_ShowChangedBySnippet = true;
_#-->
        <div class="ms-srch-hover-innerContainer ms-srch-hover-standardSize" id="_#= $htmlEncode(id + HP.ids.inner) =#_">
            <div class="ms-srch-hover-arrowBorder" id="_#= $htmlEncode(id + HP.ids.arrowBorder) =#_"></div>
            <div class="ms-srch-hover-arrow" id="_#= $htmlEncode(id + HP.ids.arrow) =#_"></div>
            <div class="ms-srch-hover-content" id="_#= $htmlEncode(id + HP.ids.content) =#_" data-displaytemplate="ProductHoverPanel">
                <div id="_#= $htmlEncode(id + HP.ids.header) =#_" class="ms-srch-hover-header">
                    _#= ctx.RenderHeader(ctx) =#_
```

Create variables for the managed properties you wish to display in the hover panel:

```
var has_name = !$isEmptyString(ctx.CurrentItem.ProductName);
var has_description = !$isEmptyString(ctx.CurrentItem.ProductDescription);
var has_color = !$isEmptyString(ctx.CurrentItem.ProductColor);
var has_listprice = !$isEmptyString(ctx.CurrentItem.ProductListPrice);
var has_category = !$isEmptyString(ctx.CurrentItem.ProductCategory);
var has_subcategory = !$isEmptyString(ctx.CurrentItem.ProductSubCategory);
```

Remove the Render Header <div>:

```
            <div class="ms-srch-hover-content" id="_#= $htmlEncode(id + HP.ids.content) =#_" data-displaytemplate
                <div id="_#= $htmlEncode(id + HP.ids.header) =#_" class="ms-srch-hover-header">
                    _#= ctx.RenderHeader(ctx) =#_
                </div>
                <div id="_#= $htmlEncode(id + HP.ids.body) =#_" class="ms-srch-hover-body">
<!--#
```

Remove the ctx.RenderBody line:

```
<div class="ms-srch-hover-innerContainer ms-srch-hover-sta
    <div class="ms-srch-hover-arrowBorder" id="_#= $htmlEn
    <div class="ms-srch-hover-arrow" id="_#= $htmlEncode(i
    <div class="ms-srch-hover-content" id="_#= $htmlEncode
        <div id="_#= $htmlEncode(id + HP.ids.header) =# "
            _#= ctx.RenderHeader(ctx) =#_
        </div>
        <div id="_#= $htmlEncode(id + HP.ids.body) =# " cl
            _#= ctx.RenderBody(ctx) =#_
        </div>
        <div id="_#= $htmlEncode(id + HP.ids.actions) =# "
            _#= ctx.RenderFooter(ctx) =#_
        </div>
    </div>
</div>
```

Again, add code blocks for each managed property. Example files are located on www.SteveTheManMann.com:

```
<div id="_#= $htmlEncode(id + HP.ids.body) =# " class="ms-srch-hover-body">

    if(has_name == true) {

        <div id="ProductNameField">
            <div id="ProductNameValue" class="ms-srch-ellipsis" style="font-weight:bold"
        </div>

    }

    if(has_description == true) {

        <div id="ProductDescriptionField">
            <div id="ProductDescriptionValue" class="ms-srch-ellipsis" title="_#= ctx.Cur
        </div>

    }

    if(has_color == true) {

        <div id="ProductColorField">
            <div id="ProductColorValue" class="ms-srch-ellipsis" title="_#= ctx.CurrentI
        </div>

    }
```

Save the file.

Step 14: Update the Result Type to Use the New Display Template

Navigate to your Search Center and select Site Settings from the Settings menu.

Under the Site Collection Administration section, click on the Search Result Types link:

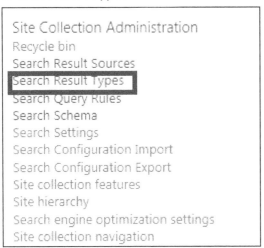

Locate the external content type Result Type and select Edit from the drop-down menu:

Change the What should these results look like? to the new display template created in the previous sections:

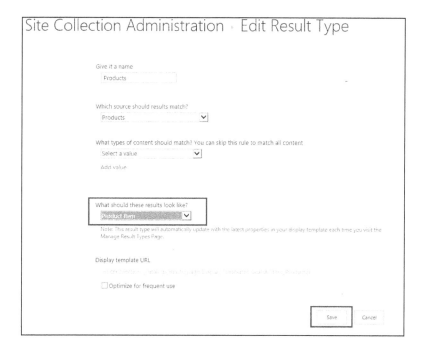

Click Save.

Step 15: Test the Item Display Template and Hover Panel

Navigate to your Search Center and perform a search within the new results page:

Product Number: SO-B909-M
Product Name: Mountain Bike Socks, M
Product Model: Mountain Bike Socks
Product Category: Clothing

Product Number: SO-B909-L
Product Name: Mountain Bike Socks, L
Product Model: Mountain Bike Socks
Product Category: Clothing

Product Number: BK-R93R-62
Product Name: Road-150 Red, 62
Product Model: Road-150
Product Category: Bikes

Product Number: BK-R93R-44
Product Name: Road-150 Red, 44
Product Model: Road-150
Product Category: Bikes

Product Number: BK-R93R-48
Product Name: Road-150 Red, 48
Product Model: Road-150
Product Category: Bikes

Road-150 Red, 62
This bike is ridden by race winners. Developed with the
Adventure Works Cycles professional race team, it has a
extremely light heat-treated aluminum frame, and steering
that allows precision control.

Color: Red
List Price: 3578.27
Product Category: Bikes
Product SubCategory: Road Bikes

OPEN   SEND

The results are shown with the managed property values and the hover panel displays additional information.

Conclusion

This guide demonstrated an end-to-end solution involving the integration of external data from SQL Server into SharePoint 2013 leveraging Business Data Connectivity Services. I hope you found this guide helpful and easy to follow. If there are any questions, issues, or concerns, please send them to steve@stevethemanmann.com.

www.ingramcontent.com/pod-product-compliance
Lightning Source LLC
Chambersburg PA
CBHW061032050326

40689CB00012B/2789